Biography

Arnold SCHWARZENEGGER

Colleen A. Sexton

A&E

Lerner Publications Company
Minneapolis

This book is available in two editions:
Library binding (0–8225–1634–9) by Lerner Publications Company,
   a division of Lerner Publishing Group
Soft cover in Spanish (0–8225–5328–7) by First Avenue Editions,
   an imprint of Lerner Publishing Group
241 First Avenue North
Minneapolis, MN 55401 U.S.A.

Website address: www.lernerbooks.com
                 www.biography.com

Library of Congress Cataloging-in-Publication Data

Sexton, Colleen A., 1967–
   Arnold Schwarzenegger / Colleen A. Sexton.
      p.   cm. — (A&E biography)
   Includes bibliographical references and index.
   Contents: Growing up—Building a champion—To America—Going
Hollywood—Fame, fortune, and politics—Governor Schwarzenegger.
      ISBN: 0-8225-1634-9 (lib. bdg. : alk. paper)
      ISBN: 0-8225-2223-3 (pbk. : alk. paper)
   1. Schwarzenegger, Schwarzenegger—Juvenile literature.
   2. Governors—California—Biography—Juvenile literature.
   3. California—Politics and government—1951—Juvenile literature.
   4. Bodybuilders—United States—Biography—Juvenile literature.
   5. Actors—United States—Biography—Juvenile literature.
   [1. Schwarzenegger, Schwarzenegger. 2. Governors. 3. Actors and
actresses. 4. Bodybuilders.] I. Title. II. Series: Biography (Lerner
Publications Company)
   F866.4.S38S48   2005
   979.4'054'092—dc22   2003025884

Manufactured in the United States of America
1 2 3 4 5 6 – JR – 10 09 08 07 06 05

CONTENTS

Arnold Schwarzenegger and his wife, Maria Shriver, celebrate the news that he won the October 2003 recall election to become the governor of California.

INTRODUCTION

Television satellite trucks lined the street outside the Century Plaza Hotel in Los Angeles, California, on October 7, 2003. People had been streaming into the hotel all evening. Inside, eighty cameras from around the world were ready to record history. The hum of the crowd rose as hundreds of people packed into the hotel ballroom. With great excitement, they awaited the arrival of their newly elected governor, Arnold Schwarzenegger.

Throughout the day, Californians had gone to the polls to make a historic decision. Should they eject their current governor, Gray Davis, from office? And if so, who should be the next governor? California's economy was troubled. Many people, including Schwarzenegger, blamed Davis, saying he had mismanaged the state's budget. Well over a million Californians had signed a petition asking for this special recall vote to determine whether or not Davis should keep his job as governor.

A field of 135 candidates emerged to oppose Davis, and from the beginning, Schwarzenegger was one of the front-runners. In a whirlwind two-month campaign, Schwarzenegger talked with Californians of all ages and backgrounds. He told them that the current government lacked leadership, that it was spending too much money and hurting the future of California.

Arnold Schwarzenegger shakes hands with his supporters on the campaign trail.

He promised to take charge of the state's budget problems. "If you want to change this state, then join me," Schwarzenegger said. When voters went to the polls, they ousted Davis and soundly elected Arnold Schwarzenegger as the leader of the most populous state in the country.

Schwarzenegger's family, friends, and supporters had gathered to celebrate this great victory. When he entered the ballroom, the crowd exploded in applause. Schwarzenegger stepped up to the podium and flashed a wide smile. He stood basking in triumph before quieting the crowd for his victory speech. Schwarzenegger thanked Californians. "I will not fail you. I will not disappoint you. And I will not let you down," he said. "I want to be the governor for the people. I want to represent everybody." As balloons and confetti filled the air, the crowd roared its approval of their new governor.

AN UNCOMMON CANDIDATE

This had not been an ordinary election, and Schwarzenegger was not an ordinary candidate. He was a political outsider—a bodybuilder, movie star, and business owner. He was not someone who had

Two young Schwarzenegger supporters hold up photos of Arnold from his bodybuilding days.

spent a lifetime in politics. He did not even look like a typical political candidate. Under his suit was the broad, muscular physique that had made him famous. Tan and well groomed, with a trim, athletic form, he was the California ideal of health and vigor.

Schwarzenegger did not sound like a typical candidate, either. His heavily accented and sometimes awkward English gave away the fact that he was an immigrant. The native Austrian had arrived in California in 1968 at age twenty-one with only twenty dollarsin his pocket. A self-made man who went on to

Schwarzenegger is a hero in Austria, especially in his home state of Styria. His image appears on the side of a house in Graz, Styria's largest city. It says "Real. Strong. Styrian."

Schwarzenegger speaks with residents and business owners of Santa Clarita, California, during his campaign for governor.

earn a fortune, Schwarzenegger appealed to California's immigrant population. On the campaign trail, he found common ground with many other citizens who had come to America to start a new life.

And Schwarzenegger certainly had more charisma and charm than the usual political candidate. With a confident grin, he tossed out the type of one-liners that had made him a popular action-movie hero. The fact that he was an actor did not stop Californians from voting for him. The state had seen its share of celebrities-turned-politicians. Sonny Bono, who had been part of the 1970s singing duo Sonny and Cher, became a U.S. senator. The residents of Carmel, California, elected actor Clint Eastwood as their mayor. And actor Ronald Reagan served as California's governor before he was elected president of the United States in 1980.

Schwarzenegger had the savvy of a salesperson. He would sell himself to the voters and then sell California to the world. He told voters that, unlike a career politician, he was a successful business owner who knew how to manage a budget. He assured the state's residents that he would be a strong leader who would responsibly guide California, one of the world's largest and most diverse economies.

The family members who surrounded Schwarzenegger on stage that night also made him an unusual candidate. His wife, Maria Shriver, is the niece of former U.S. president John F. Kennedy. The Kennedys are one of America's most legendary families, with members famous for their Democratic politics and liberal causes. Schwarzenegger is the lone Republican among them, differing mainly in his more conservative economic views. On social issues such as education and the environment, however, he mostly agrees with the Kennedy clan. This mix of views appealed to Californians looking for a moderate candidate.

Throughout his life, Schwarzenegger had built his career by reinventing himself—from bodybuilder to actor to entrepreneur. Now he would need to reinvent himself again as Governor Schwarzenegger. Although

Maria (right) *and her parents, Eunice* (left) *and Sargent Shriver* (second from left), *celebrate Schwarzenegger's victory with him after the results of the California gubernatorial recall election are announced.*

he had never before held political office and knew little about the legislative process, Schwarzenegger was confident in his ability to govern. He would approach his new mission the same way he had approached every goal in his life—with fierce determination. From the beginning, failure had never been an option for Arnold Schwarzenegger.

Arnold grew up in the village of Thal, Austria.

Chapter **ONE**

GROWING UP

THE STORY OF ARNOLD ALOIS SCHWARZENEGGER began in the small Austrian village of Thal. Nestled among forested hills and sparkling lakes, Thal lies only a few miles from Graz, Austria's second largest city. It was in this scenic southeastern region of the country that the Schwarzeneggers put down roots generations ago.

Arnold's father, Gustav, came from a modest family of locksmiths and steelworkers. Even as a child, Gustav stood out from the rest of his family for his wit, charm, and good looks. As an adult, "he was always neat, his hair slicked back, his mustache trimmed to a line," Arnold remembered. Gustav played six instruments, and music was his lifelong joy. He also carried himself with an almost military bearing and was drawn to a life of discipline. As a young man, Gustav became a member of the Austrian police force. For years to come, he would fuel his love of music by playing in the Graz police band.

In 1938 military troops from neighboring Germany seized control of Austria and united it with Germany. Along with many other Austrians, Gustav welcomed German rule. They hoped it would mean a better economic future for Austria. Gustav joined the Nazi Party, the political group headed by Germany's leader, Adolf Hitler. Under Hitler's rule, the German army invaded much of Europe during World War II (1939–1945) and exterminated millions of Jews (an event known as the Holocaust). Although there are no existing records of his war service, Gustav reportedly

A FATHER'S PAST

Concerned about his father's activities for the Nazis during World War II, Schwarzenegger once asked the Simon Wiesenthal Center in Los Angeles to investigate Gustav Schwarzenegger. The center works to keep the memory of the Holocaust alive. Researchers found no evidence that Gustav was directly involved in sending Jews to Nazi concentration camps to be killed.

Arnold's family lived in the top floor of this house while the children were growing up.

served in Germany's military police and was stationed in Belgium during the war.

On October 20, 1945, shortly after the war ended with Germany's defeat, thirty-eight-year-old Gustav married a twenty-three-year-old widow named Aurelia Jadrny. Dark-haired with front teeth that stuck out slightly, Aurelia had worked in an office distributing food stamps during the war. The newlyweds moved to Thal, where Gustav took the job of police chief. With the position came living quarters on the top floor of a three-hundred-year-old stone house. The house was cold, with only wood- and coal-burning stoves for heat. There was no indoor plumbing, so Aurelia spent much of her time running up and down the stairs to bring in water from a village fountain. She cooked, sewed, and kept the house spotless while her husband went to work each day.

Although Gustav and Aurelia had pleasant and happy days, Aurelia often worried about her new husband. He had a mean temper and sometimes became violent, especially when he drank. Gathering in the local tavern for drinks and conversation was a favorite pastime for many villagers, but Gustav often drank so much that he had to be carried home.

A STRICT UPBRINGING

Within one year of their marriage, the Schwarzeneggers' first son was born. Meinhard arrived on July 17, 1946. One year later, on July 30, 1947, his little brother Arnold was born. From the start, Meinhard was Gustav's favorite son, a strong, handsome, and outgoing boy. Arnold, on the other hand, was often ill as a child. His ears stuck out, and he wore thick glasses. Shy and anxious, Arnold was especially afraid of his strict father.

Gustav strongly believed in discipline and set out to instill it in his sons. He believed his boys would gain strength and power by enduring pain and hardship. "He had no patience for listening to understand your problems," Arnold recalled. There was a military-like routine to the brothers' daily lives. The boys were required to keep their clothes clean and neat, their shoes free of dirt. On weekdays, the brothers woke up early in the morning to do chores. They walked to a nearby farm for fresh milk and fetched water and firewood. When it snowed, the brothers shoveled the paths around their house before heading off to school. The boys also attended religious studies during the week, and every Sunday the family went together to the local Roman Catholic church.

Weekends brought trips to neighboring farms and outings to Graz to museums, plays, and concerts. But they were hard for the boys to enjoy, because they knew that at the end of each weekend excursion their father would give them an assignment. "We would have to write an essay about what we had learned. I mean, a lot of fun, right?" Arnold said. Then Gustav would read, correct, and grade the required ten-page essay, marking any mistakes in red pencil. He would not accept errors, and a misspelled word often brought the punishment of writing out the correct spelling fifty times. Arnold almost always made more mistakes than Meinhard and had to face his father's scorn.

Gustav considered athletic training important. He himself was a champion at amateur curling, a sport in which teams slide large stones across ice. From an early age, Meinhard and Arnold were regularly swimming, hiking, bicycling, and running. When Arnold was six years old, Gustav took him to Graz to see the famous American Olympic swimmer and movie star Johnny Weissmuller dedicate a new swimming pool. For the first time, young Arnold dreamed of becoming a great athlete.

Young Arnold admired Olympic swimmer Johnny Weissmuller, who played Tarzan in the movies.

Competition was part of Arnold and Meinhard's lives from the beginning. Gustav made almost every activity a contest. He set the boys against each other, exclaiming, "Let's see who's the best!" Whether it was in foot races or ski races, in boxing matches, or in the everyday drudgery of studying and chores, Arnold constantly competed with his brother for his father's approval. But Arnold was almost always second best in his father's eyes.

Aurelia, on the other hand, always tried to treat her sons equally. She set up a daily routine for both boys to follow and carefully watched over their health as they grew. She listened to their problems and showed them some of the kindness and love lacking in their relationship with their father. A traditional housewife, Aurelia worked hard to keep a pleasant home for her family.

LIFE IN THAL

Although the Schwarzenegger household was disciplined and orderly, the same could not be said for Austria after World War II. The Allies—led by Great Britain, the Soviet Union, and the United States—had defeated the Germans. Austria was reestablished as an independent country, but its economy was in ruins. The Schwarzeneggers were among many who struggled to make ends meet. They rarely had meat to eat, except for an occasional Sunday treat of Wiener schnitzel, a traditional Austrian dish. The family had to go to the local inn to use a telephone. "We had no flushing toilet in the house. No refrigerator. No television. What we did have was food rations—and we did have British tanks around to give us kids an occasional lift to the elementary school," Arnold remembered.

One of the high points of Arnold's childhood was the day the family bought a refrigerator. "When it came, I remember, we were all standing around the kitchen looking at it," Arnold said. "Then my mother opened it up, and we all stuck our hands in there, and it was cold, and we were freaking out like this was the strangest thing you could imagine."

When he was allowed some free time, Arnold listened to the radio for entertainment. He and his friends hiked in the woods around Thal and gathered at the local lake, where they ice-skated in winter and boated in summer. They had swimming races and dove to the bottom of the lake to collect handfuls of

Arnold and his friends spent a lot of time swimming, ice skating, and playing games at this lake in Thal.

mud for mudball fights. Some days after school, children in the neighborhood gathered in a field across from the Schwarzenegger house to play soccer, badminton, volleyball, and other games.

At school, Arnold was an average student who showed a talent for drawing. He became known for his sense of humor and funny pranks. He could also be a bully at times, especially when egged on by Meinhard. The brothers teased and fought with their classmates. One day, Meinhard and Arnold even ganged up on an adult, a milkman. Gustav settled the matter quietly, showing his own power as police chief. His refusal to punish Meinhard and Arnold only encouraged his sons to dominate others. A bigger and meaner bully than his younger brother, Meinhard was eventually expelled and sent to reform school.

ARNOLD'S DREAM

Young Arnold channeled much of his energy into sports. At age ten, he joined the Graz Athletic Club and played wing position on the soccer team for nearly five years. But team sports did not always satisfy Arnold. He didn't want to share the spotlight with his teammates. He wanted to stand out and be recognized as the best. So he took up individual sports, including swimming, boxing, and gymnastics, as well as shot put and javelin throwing. But none of these sports felt right.

One day his soccer coach took the team to a bodybuilding gym to train with weights. The coach wanted his players to strengthen their legs. Arnold was thirteen years old, and it was the first time he had seen anyone lift weights. He stood in awe, watching the powerfully built men flex their huge muscles. "And there it was before me—my life, the answer I'd been seeking," Arnold recalled. "It was something I suddenly just seemed to reach out and find, as if I'd been crossing a suspended bridge and finally stepped off onto solid ground." Arnold was hooked from the first moment he touched the weights. He wanted to be a bodybuilder.

Arnold spent hours poring over American bodybuilding magazines, where champions such as Steve

Reeves, Larry Scott, and Ray Routledge popped off the pages. In one of these magazines, Arnold found his hero, Reg Park, a huge and rugged English body-builder. "That's what I wanted to be, ultimately: big," remembered Arnold. "Reg Park was the epitome of that dream, the biggest, most powerful person in bodybuilding."

Arnold was impressed by the way the men in the magazines had shaped and molded their bodies. He began to study anatomy, learning the names of the various muscles: bicep, tricep, pectoral, trapezius. He put up pictures of Reg Park in his room and memorized the size and proportion of Park's arms, legs, and chest. He found out how Park trained, what he ate, and how he lived.

This photo of Reg Park and his daughter was taken in 1956. Arnold admired Reg Park for his bodybuilding image and movie star status.

Arnold was also spending more time at the movies, where Reg Park, Steve Reeves, and other bodybuilders came alive on the screen in action and adventure films. In a series of movies, Reg Park played Hercules, a hero from ancient Greek mythology known for his great strength. Sitting in a dark theater, Arnold studied the way his hero moved across the screen. He became determined to build his body the way Reg Park had. One day, Arnold believed, he would be the best bodybuilder in the world.

Arnold also dreamed of the United States, where everything was big. From the towering skyscrapers of crowded cities to the hulking cars that cruised down wide, endless highways, Arnold loved the America he saw in magazines and movies. "I want to be there!" he told himself. "I want to be part of it!" Although he was barely even a teenager, Arnold set out to fulfill his dreams.

A young Arnold Schwarzenegger struts his stuff.

Chapter **TWO**

BUILDING A CHAMPION

AFTER COMPLETING HIS FIRST REAL WORKOUT WITH weights, Arnold was excited and happy. He climbed onto his bike in Graz and started pedaling the eight miles home. He thought about how much he loved the clanking sound of the metal weights and the smell of sweat in the gym. Suddenly, all feeling left his legs and he tumbled off his bike. Arnold had trained so hard that his body was weak and numb. He picked himself up and tried to ride again, but he couldn't do it. Leaning heavily on his bike, Arnold pushed it the rest of the way home to Thal. His muscles were so sore the next morning that he couldn't raise his arm high enough to comb his hair.

Instead of discouraging him, the soreness made Arnold want to work harder. "I learned that this pain

Kurt Marnul (right) *was Arnold's weight lifting mentor at a Marnul's gym in Graz, Austria.*

meant progress," he said. "Each time my muscles were sore from a workout, I knew they were growing." By age fifteen, he was training six days a week at Graz's only weight lifting gym. Kurt Marnul, a champion bodybuilder who had started the gym, became Arnold's mentor. Arnold relied on Marnul for guidance on training and nutrition. And Marnul often provided the young bodybuilder with a warm meal, a hot shower, and rides home to Thal.

Soon Arnold was working out two hours a day, then four hours a day. He watched his muscles grow, amazed that he could change his body in that way. Arnold set a goal. He would bulk up his skinny six-foot-tall, 150-pound frame to a massive 250 pounds. Arnold wanted to become the biggest and the best bodybuilder on the planet. "I could see how he wanted to reach higher goals," Marnul remembered. "If it would have been up to Arnold, he would have taken his weights to bed with him."

THE BODYBUILDER AT HOME

At home in Thal, Arnold's parents were worried about their son. He did not care about anything except bodybuilding. He was emotionally distant. He stopped going to church, and his schoolwork suffered. Aurelia was afraid he would hurt himself, while Gustav thought it was not normal for a boy to be so obsessed with weight lifting. They asked what he planned to do with his future. Arnold answered that he was going to become the world's best-built man and then go to the United States to act in movies. Gustav shook his head at this news. He decided Arnold should stay at home more and limited his son's trips to Graz to three times a week. Arnold agreed but then set up a gym at home.

Three nights a week, Arnold biked to Graz to train at the gym. The other nights, he trained at home. Karl Gerstl, a local doctor and enthusiastic weight lifter, became Arnold's first training partner. Barbell curls, bench presses, squats, chin-ups, and other exercises were helping Arnold build up his muscles quickly. Gerstl made daily training a competition, giving Arnold the drive to be tougher and work harder. He also got Arnold thinking about the power the mind could have over the body.

As Arnold's muscles grew, so did his confidence and his ego. Among his friends and neighbors, Arnold was finally getting the attention he had always wanted. They were impressed with his athletic body. Classmates volunteered to help him with his homework. Neighbors offered milk, eggs, and vegetables to fuel his workouts. And girls looked at him in a new way. Arnold enjoyed the attention, and it motivated him to continue working hard.

But not all the attention he received was positive. When Arnold asked a girl he liked out on a date, she laughed and said no. She thought he was in love with himself and spent too much time looking in the mirror. "Nobody seemed to understand what was involved in body-building," Arnold recalled. "You do look at your body in a mirror, not because you are narcissistic, but because you are trying to check your progress." Some people made fun of him. They asked why he would want to pursue such an unpopular sport, one in which only a few dozen Austrians participated. All Arnold could say was that he loved it.

Despite his obsessive dedication to bodybuilding, Arnold did make quick ventures into other sports. He won Austria's junior national curling championship when he was seventeen years old, the same year his father won the senior title. Arnold also won

This gym in Graz, where Arnold began his bodybuilding career, has been turned into the Arnold Schwarzenegger Museum.

the first-place trophy from the Austrian Junior Weight Lifting Championship.

Gustav and Aurelia were pleased with Arnold's accomplishments and boasted to their friends and neighbors about their strong and talented son. Finally, Arnold had earned his father's praise. But Gustav and Aurelia still worried about Arnold's future. They wanted him to settle down and get a good job.

IN THE ARMY

In October 1965, just a few months after his eighteenth birthday, Schwarzenegger joined the Austrian army. All able-bodied Austrian men were required to serve one year in the military. Schwarzenegger, attracted to the size and power of tanks, had told his father how much he wanted to drive the vehicles. Gustav pulled some strings, and Schwarzenegger was assigned to a tank unit stationed near Graz. The army usually required their tank drivers to be at least twenty-one years old, but they made an exception for Schwarzenegger. Gustav hoped his son's army experience would lead to a career in the military.

Schwarzenegger liked the army. He was used to leading a disciplined life and adjusted easily to the rules and daily regimen of the army. He enjoyed wearing a uniform every day and appreciated the regular meals. For the first time in his life, he was eating meat at every meal and getting the protein his body needed to gain muscle mass.

Soon after starting his army service, however, Schwarzenegger was faced with a dilemma. He received an invitation to the Junior Mr. Europe contest in Stuttgart, Germany. But he was in the middle of basic training and was forbidden to leave camp. Schwarzenegger decided he could not miss the competition. Not caring about the consequences, he climbed over the wall that surrounded the base and hopped on a train to Germany.

It was Schwarzenegger's first major bodybuilding competition, and he was nervous as he stepped in front of the judges. At bodybuilding events, contestants strike poses that show off certain muscles. Schwarzenegger knew little about posing except what he had seen in bodybuilding magazines. He decided to strike the poses he had seen in photographs of Reg Park. It worked. The judges announced that Arnold Schwarzenegger was the new Mr. Europe Junior. "I felt like King Kong," Schwarzenegger remembered. "I loved the sudden attention. I strutted and flexed."

The army was not as happy about his big win as Schwarzenegger was. Guards caught him as he returned to base, and he was put in the camp jail for seven days. But word of Schwarzenegger's adventure spread through the camp. Many soldiers—including some influential officers—saw him as a hero, an athlete who could bring pride to Austria. He soon received an order to spend his afternoons on bodybuilding. The army even set up a gym where he trained six hours a day. By the time his year of service was up, Schwarzenegger had packed on another twenty-five pounds of muscle.

As he left the army in 1966, Schwarzenegger felt he was free. His life was his own, and he could go anywhere. What he wanted most was to get out of Austria. The country was too small for him. "It wouldn't allow me to expand. There seemed never to be enough space. Even people's ideas were small," he remembered. He knew bodybuilding was his ticket to bigger and better things.

A New Life

Schwarzenegger had a plan. At the Junior Mr. Europe contest, a German man named Putziger had approached him. Putziger owned a magazine and a gym in Munich, Germany, and he wanted Schwarzenegger to manage the gym. Putziger promised Schwarzenegger that he could train all he wanted and would get an airplane ticket to London to watch the Mr. Universe contest. Schwarzenegger took Putziger up on his offer. But Schwarzenegger said he would compete, not just watch.

When Schwarzenegger stepped off the train in Munich, he was met by the bustle of a big city. The tall buildings, sounds of traffic, and especially the crowds overwhelmed him. He had never seen so many different kinds of people who spoke so many different languages. And everyone was in a hurry to get somewhere.

Schwarzenegger rented a room and went to work at Putziger's gym, doing anything that was needed, including mopping floors and cleaning bathrooms. His main job, however, was to develop training programs for people who wanted to get in shape. At first, Schwarzenegger felt awkward when clients turned to him for guidance. After all, he thought, he still needed advice on his own workouts. Being an instructor was also frustrating because clients took away time that he could spend training. "They merely went through the motions, doing sissy workouts, pampering themselves," Schwarzenegger remembered. "And there was so much I wanted to do with those wasted hours."

To fit his training around his job, Schwarzenegger split his workout routine. He worked on his arms and shoulders for two hours in the morning and his chest, abdominals, and legs for two hours at night. In between, he ate two heavy meals. Schwarzenegger found that by breaking up his routine, he had more energy to tackle each workout and could lift more weight. Within two months, he had added five more pounds of muscle to his frame. Later, Schwarzenegger's split workout would become famous, and bodybuilders around the world would make it their standard routine.

Schwarzenegger's training partner in Munich was Franco Columbu, a power weigh tlifter from the Italian island of Sardinia. Schwarzenegger and Columbu first met in Stuttgart, Germany, at the Mr. Europe Junior contest. Working together in Munich, the two became close friends.

During his workouts with Columbu, Schwarzenegger pushed himself hard and found he was bulking up fast. Lifting weights simply made him happier than anything else did. With each repetition, or "rep," he could feel the blood surge to the muscle he was working. This "pump" gave him a rush, the feeling that keeps bodybuilders going.

Schwarzenegger began entering powerlifting contests with Columbu. He wanted people to know that his muscles were not just for show—he was strong too. From the start, Schwarzenegger had trained the muscles he

Schwarzenegger (right) *and Columbu* (left) *striking bodybuilding poses in the 1970s. The two men met and became friends while training together in Munich, Germany.*

needed for heavy lifting. At the 1966 International Powerlifting Championship, Columbu took the middleweight title. Schwarzenegger won too, taking the heavyweight title after lifting a total of 1,745 pounds in three types of lifts—485 pounds in the bench press, 550 pounds in the squat, and 710 pounds in the dead lift.

By this time, Schwarzenegger had developed the confidence and charm—and aggressiveness—of someone who knows he is a winner. He often took this attitude out on the town in Munich. He and Columbu spent their free time dating women and hanging out in the city's beer halls and restaurants. Over giant steins of beer, Schwarzenegger entertained friends with stories. Often he took out his aggression in barroom brawls, earning a reputation as a fighter. He gained fame among his buddies as a bad and dangerous driver who racked up a lot of speeding tickets.

Schwarzenegger also became a legendary practical joker who preyed on people's weaknesses. He convinced eager bodybuilders to go on diets of ice cream or sugar cubes or salt—none of which would help them and could possibly hurt them. He told one bodybuilder that the latest trend among U.S. bodybuilders was to scream while posing in competitions. The man tried it and looked like a fool.

THE BUSINESS OF COMPETING

Schwarzenegger's rowdy activities did not distract him from his immediate goals. He entered and won the titles of Mr. Europe and the Best-Built Man of Europe. He was all ready to make a run at the top spot—Mr. Universe—when he learned that funding for his ticket to London had fallen through. Friends and supporters spent the next month raising money for his trip. Schwarzenegger was nervous when it came time to leave. He'd never been on an airplane before. "I remember thinking as I did up my seatbelt, 'What if it crashes and I never get there?'" Schwarzenegger recalled. "And when I heard the landing gear come up with a shudder into the body of the plane, it was like a cold fist closing on my heart. I was certain we were gone." At age nineteen, he was about to experience his first international bodybuilding contest.

In London Schwarzenegger checked out the competition. When he saw the smooth, tan U.S. bodybuilder Chet Yorton, he knew he could not win. Schwarzenegger had huge, rugged muscles, but Yorton had gone one step further. Each of his muscles was "cut," or defined. The muscles rippled with veins, showing that he had little fat under his skin. Watching Yorton, Schwarzenegger knew that he needed to polish his bulky muscles. "That was mere foundation material," he said. "I had to get the separation, the finish, the tan." Schwarzenegger saw that he had a lot to learn about posing too. He watched other top bodybuilders flow in a rhythm from one pose to another or shift to each pose with a pop, showing off their muscles in the best way possible. Finally, Schwarzenegger realized that he had to work on his legs and calves. In Europe, building the upper body was key. But to be a world champion, he needed bulk and definition in his legs. After taking an unexpected second in the Mr. Universe competition, Schwarzenegger went back to Munich and back to his workouts with a new determination.

Schwarzenegger's parents still did not understand why their son insisted on being a bodybuilder. They wanted him to come back to Thal and get a real job. He was still finding it hard to make ends meet in Munich, but he was careful not to let his parents know. When the owner of the gym he managed offered to sell it to Schwarzenegger, he jumped at the chance. He borrowed money and took other jobs to scrape together the funds he needed. He used his celebrity as a bodybuilder to attract people to his gym, eventually gaining hundreds of new members. In a short time, Schwarzenegger paid off his debts and began to make a profit. At age twenty, Schwarzenegger was a business owner. And he knew that having a good head for business was important for his future.

In the fall of 1966, Schwarzenegger received a call from Wag Bennett, a gym owner in London who had been one of the judges at the Mr. Universe contest. Bennett was impressed with Schwarzenegger and wanted him to tour Britain in a bodybuilding exhibition. Schwarzenegger agreed, and Bennett took the young bodybuilder under his wing. He taught Schwarzenegger how to pose effectively and suggested he develop a routine set to music from *Exodus,* a popular movie. "He showed me how to hit the best, most dramatic poses during the high points of the music and how to do the less dramatic, more subtle poses during the quieter parts," remembered Schwarzenegger. The response to this new routine was overwhelming, and his confidence grew. Schwarzenegger went on to tour in Belgium and the Netherlands and learned more about the business of bodybuilding. He was self-assured on stage and knew how to appeal to an audience. Newspapers gave him nicknames such as the Giant of Austria and the Austrian Oak. He was becoming a bodybuilding star.

In January 1967, one of Schwarzenegger's childhood dreams came true. He met his idol, Reg Park. They went on a weeklong exhibition tour through Britain and worked out together every day. Schwarzenegger took the opportunity to learn all he could from Park. He took notes, and when he returned to Munich, he changed his workout routine according to what he'd learned. Park predicted that Schwarzenegger would be the next Mr. Universe and made a deal with him. If Schwarzenegger won the contest, Park would bring him on an exhibition tour through South Africa, where Park lived.

MR. UNIVERSE

Schwarzenegger was favored to win the 1967 Mr. Universe title. He weighed about 250 pounds, his muscles were cut, and he was in top form. He was mentally prepared too, having visualized his victory over and over in his mind. He knew his biggest competition would be Dennis Tinnerino, who had just won the Mr. America contest. Everyone who had seen Tinnerino told Schwarzenegger the American would be tough to beat.

Bodybuilding competitions are broken down into two parts. The first afternoon is the prejudging, which is attended only by judges, the press, and other bodybuilders. Judges line up the bodybuilders and separate them into short, medium, and tall classes. They then watch the bodybuilders pose in groups and individually. The next evening's competition takes place in front of an audience. The judges announce the top winner from each class, and those three bodybuilders compete for the top prize.

Schwarzenegger and Tinnerino were both in the tall class, and Schwarzenegger deliberately lined up next to Tinnerino for the prejudging. He wanted the judges to compare them side by side. "I knew I could upstage him," Schwarzenegger remembered. "I felt good. My body was pumped and tight, blood surging out to

STEROIDS

Schwarzenegger has admitted to using steroids during his bodybuilding career. In fact, he started taking them on the advice of the bodybuilders he first trained with. They said the drugs gave bodybuilders a competitive edge. At that time, no one knew how dangerous steroids could be.

Anabolic steroids are made from the male hormone testosterone. The human body naturally produces testosterone, but steroids greatly increase testosterone levels in the body. Steroids can help athletes build muscle tissue and increase strength. But today we know that they can also cause liver damage, depression, high blood pressure, and aggressive behavior. Most sports competitions now prohibit the use of steroids and do regular testing of athletes to make sure they aren't breaking the rules.

There's no doubt that using steroids helped Schwarzenegger bulk up. But steroids alone could not make him a champion. What he achieved required hard work and dedication. Today, he condemns the use of steroids and says that if he had known then what he knows now, he never would have taken them.

every capillary. I just felt that there was no way Tinnerino could beat me." After the initial posing, the judges chose six men for a pose-off. Out of the corner of his eye, Schwarzenegger watched Tinnerino carefully, always making sure he struck a more dramatic pose than the American did.

The next night, the crowd roared when Schwarzenegger started posing. "Arnold! Arnold!" they shouted. When the judges announced the winner of each class, they called Schwarzenegger's name. He had beat Tinnerino in the tall class. The crowd went wild and quieted only long enough for the judges to declare that Schwarzenegger was Mr. Universe 1967. "I heard my name and stepped up on the platform," Schwarzenegger recalled. "The applause was like thunder roaring through the auditorium. People were shouting and clamoring. I looked at the lineup of bodybuilders and said to myself, 'My god, I did it. I beat them all.'" At age twenty, Schwarzenegger was the youngest Mr. Universe ever.

Schwarzenegger was amazed. He had accomplished his goal, he thought. He was the best bodybuilder in the world. But that was not exactly true. He had won one of three Mr. Universe titles—the National Amateur British Bodybuilding Association (NABBA) amateur title. There was also the NABBA professional Mr. Universe champion and the International Federation of Bodybuilders (IFBB) Mr. Universe title. He realized he still had many challenges ahead.

Schwarzenegger pretends to drink from his 1967 Mr. Universe trophy while at dinner with friends to celebrate his victory.

After visiting Reg Park in South Africa as they had agreed, Schwarzenegger headed home to Munich. His gym was flourishing, and he began taking business classes. He also hit the weights harder than ever, training for two and a half hours, twice a day. He especially targeted his calves and other muscles he considered his weak spots. The training paid off. In September 1968, he won the NABBA professional Mr. Universe competition. In his mind, his next stop was clear: America and the IFBB Mr. Universe contest.

By the time Schwarzenegger was twenty-one, he had won eight weight lifting and bodybuilding titles, including NABBA Mr. Universe.

Chapter **THREE**

TO AMERICA

To Schwarzenegger, the United States was the land of winners. And he wanted to know why. What did American bodybuilders know that he did not? In 1968 Schwarzenegger finally had the opportunity to find out. Joe Weider, a muscle magazine publisher, invited Schwarzenegger to Miami, Florida, to compete in the IFBB Mr. Universe competition.

Schwarzenegger wowed the crowd at the IFBB Mr. Universe contest. When he spread out his massive muscles, the audience cheered and shouted his name. They had never seen such a big bodybuilder. But bulk was not enough to win. Schwarzenegger lost to Frank Zane, whose muscles had better definition, the judges ruled. The defeat shook Schwarzenegger's confidence.

"I remember the words that kept going through my head: 'I'm away from home, in this strange city, in America, and I'm a loser...,'" Schwarzenegger said. "I cried all night because of it. I had disappointed all my friends, everybody, especially myself. It was awful. I felt it was the end of the world."

Weider, on the other hand, saw only potential in Schwarzenegger and offered him a deal. Weider would set him up in Santa Monica, California, for one year with an apartment, a car, and one hundred dollars a week. In exchange, Schwarzenegger would provide information about his training regimen and allow his photographs to be used in Weider's magazines. Schwarzenegger agreed.

Faced with nothing but free time, Schwarzenegger was determined to train hard to beat all the American body-builders. He worked out at the famous Gold's Gym in Venice, California, where all the top bodybuilders trained. To acquire the suntan all competitors desired, he ran on the beach and swam in the ocean. He focused on sculpting his muscles, rather than on bulking up. Soon he had chiseled himself down from 250 pounds to 230 pounds, and his muscles were defined and deeply veined.

The summer of 1969 brought another new experience. Schwarzenegger started his first serious romantic relationship. He began dating Barbara Outland, a student at San Diego State University. She was working as a waitress over the summer at a Santa Monica restaurant. Until he met Barbara, Schwarzenegger had dated just for fun, never seeing a future with any of the women he met. But Barbara was different. Her warmth and spirit impressed Schwarzenegger, and he had great respect for her.

PLAYING HERCULES

Now that he was in the United States, Schwarzenegger was one step closer to his dream of acting in the movies. An Italian television production company was casting a movie called *Hercules Goes Bananas,* to be filmed in New York. The company contacted Weider looking for a bodybuilder to play Hercules, the same Greek hero that Reg Park had played years ago. Weider told the film-makers that Schwarzenegger was perfect for the job. Schwarzenegger's Austrian accent did not even matter, because the film would be dubbed into Italian.

Schwarzenegger auditioned and won the role. He was thrilled. He had only been in the United States a few months and already he was in the movies. For his twelve weeks of filming, Schwarzenegger would be paid twelve thousand dollars.

Schwarzenegger acted under the stage name Arnold Strong for his movie debut. In the film, the god Zeus sends his son Hercules to New York City as punishment. Once there, Hercules is chased by beautiful women, battles gangsters, and becomes a professional wrestler. The movie ends with a chariot race through Times Square. Although the movie had a ridiculous storyline and was poorly directed, Schwarzenegger

Schwarzenegger (right) *made his Hollywood debut playing* Hercules in Hercules in New York. *He was on his way to achieving his boyhood dream.*

stood out in every scene. His physical presence and awkward, youthful charm were appealing.

The movie came out in 1970 in Italy. Later dubbed into English, it was released in the United States as *Hercules in New York*. Schwarzenegger invested his earnings from the movie in California real estate.

THE BEST

In the fall of 1969, Schwarzenegger flew to New York City for the IFBB Mr. Universe contest. He was prepared to face his biggest competition, Cuban bodybuilder Sergio Oliva, also known as the Myth. But Oliva wasn't there—he was competing at the Mr. Olympia contest on the other side of the city.

Schwarzenegger easily won the Mr. Universe title, placing first among all seven judges. He then bolted across town and entered the Mr. Olympia contest at the last minute, hoping to beat his rival. But when he saw the Myth, Schwarzenegger knew that Oliva was in better shape than he was. Schwarzenegger had to settle for second place.

Losing had given Schwarzenegger a new challenge. He would beat Sergio Oliva. He told Weider he would stay for another year. Schwarzenegger relied on his friend Columbu, who had come to California over the summer, to push him hard during training.

In both 1969 and 1970, Schwarzenegger won the NABBA Mr. Universe contest in London, the second time defeating his hero Reg Park, who had briefly come out of retirement. Next up was the Mr. World competition in Columbus, Ohio, where Schwarzenegger again faced Oliva. Schwarzenegger was more focused in this contest than ever before. When the judges proclaimed Oliva the second-place winner, the audience began shouting, "Arnold! Arnold!" Schwarzenegger realized he had won. "In a single second, I had taken the final step," he remembered. "I had conquered every great bodybuilder in the world."

A New Focus

With his Mr. World win, the competitive pressure was off. At age twenty-two, Schwarzenegger had proved he was the best. While he planned to continue training and competing, he also began looking for ways to make money from his success. Using his business sense and ambition, he intended to create an empire and make a fortune. Schwarzenegger would start by educating people about the sport of bodybuilding. He established a mail-order business selling photographs of himself, as well as T-shirts, posing trunks, and training guides on bodybuilding. He led seminars about the sport all over the world. Schwarzenegger knew it was important to stay in the spotlight. He also took more business classes and started a bricklaying business with Columbu.

In May 1971, Schwarzenegger received tragic news from home. After a night of drinking, his brother Meinhard had crashed his car into another vehicle. He died instantly. Meinhard left behind a three-year-old son named Patrick, Schwarzenegger's godson. Schwarzenegger resolved to help support Patrick as he grew up.

More bad news came the following year, when Gustav died of a stroke in December 1972. Schwarzenegger had seen his father just a few months earlier, when Gustav came to see him defend his Mr. Olympia title in Essen, Germany. But Schwarzenegger did not attend his father's funeral, for reasons that remain unclear. Over the years, Schwarzenegger has given various explanations: he was too deep in training, he was on vacation and out of touch, or he was in the hospital with a leg injury. Another explanation may be Schwarzenegger's lingering resentment toward his father for his difficult childhood. But Schwarzenegger also credited Gustav for creating in him a drive for success.

Wider fame was just around the corner for Schwarzenegger. He made an important connection in

1972, when he met George Butler, who planned to write a book and film a documentary about bodybuilding. Butler wanted to focus both projects on twenty-five-year-old Schwarzenegger—the biggest star in the world of bodybuilding.

As Butler and his coauthor, Charles Gaines, went to work on their project, Schwarzenegger took on another movie role. In 1973, three years after his film debut, Schwarzenegger had a minor part in *The Long Goodbye,* a major studio release. Schwarzenegger played a burly hit man working for the mob. That same year, he won his fourth straight Mr. Olympia contest.

Butler and Gaines's book, *Pumping Iron,* was published in 1974 with little fanfare. At that time, it was mostly professional athletes who worked out in gyms and lifted weights. The publisher didn't believe a general audience would buy a book about bodybuilding. The publisher didn't do much to promote *Pumping Iron,* and the *New York Times* refused to review it. But the publisher and reviewers didn't count on a growing physical fitness craze in the United States. Americans were eager to get in shape and build toned muscles. Two months after its publication date, *Pumping Iron* was a best-seller. Bodybuilding was starting to get the broad recognition that Schwarzenegger strongly believed it deserved.

Butler and Gaines were suddenly in demand for interviews. In November 1974, they had the attention of a national television audience when they sat down with Barbara Walters, then an anchor on NBC's *The*

BODYBUILDING TITLES

Year	Title	Year	Title
1965	Junior Mr. Europe	1969	IFBB Mr. Universe, amateur
1966	Best-Built Man of Europe	1969	NABBA Mr. Universe, professional
1966	Mr. Europe	1970	NABBA Mr. Universe, professional
1966	International Powerlifting Championship	1970	Mr. World
1967	NABBA Mr. Universe, amateur	1970	IFBB Mr. Olympia
1968	NABBA Mr. Universe, professional	1971	IFBB Mr. Olympia
1968	German Powerlifting Championship	1972	IFBB Mr. Olympia
		1973	IFBB Mr. Olympia
		1974	IFBB Mr. Olympia
1968	IFBB Mr. International	1975	IFBB Mr. Olympia
		1980	IFBB Mr. Olympia

Today Show. Butler and Gaines brought Schwarzenegger along for the interview. Schwarzenegger came across as sincere, confident, and knowledgeable. Walters and much of the viewing public were impressed.

Schwarzenegger's life was headed in a new direction. He and Barbara Outland had ended their relationship. She was ready to settle down, while Schwarzenegger was constantly looking for a new challenge. In fact, he was ready for a big change. After defending his Mr. Olympia title in 1974, he considered retiring from

Schwarzenegger and his mother attend the Golden Globe Awards in 1977. Schwarzenegger won a Golden Globe Award for Most Promising Newcomer to Film for Stay Hungry.

bodybuilding. But Butler was planning the second part of his *Pumping Iron* project, the documentary film. He wanted Schwarzenegger to be the star. The film would show Schwarzenegger and other body-builders as they prepared for the 1975 Mr. Olympia. Schwarzenegger decided to train for this one last competition and then announce his retirement.

Before pumping up for *Pumping Iron,* Schwarzenegger appeared in *Stay Hungry,* a movie written by Gaines that starred Jeff Bridges and Sally Field. Schwarzenegger had a major role in the film, playing a bodybuilder named Joe Santo. The movie itself didn't do well at the box office or among critics, but Schwarzenegger received high praise for his performance. In fact, he won a Golden Globe Award as Most Promising Newcomer to Film when the film was released in 1977. This, it seemed, would be a banner year for Schwarzenegger.

Schwarzenegger strikes a pose in a scene from Pumping Iron, *a documentary film about bodybuilding.*

Chapter **FOUR**

GOING HOLLYWOOD

THE SCENE IS UNEXPECTED. SCHWARZENEGGER AND HIS friend Franco Columbu stand at the bar in a ballet studio, following the movements of an instructor. Muscles bulging, the men bend gracefully and sweep their arms in the air. Ballet classes were helping them polish their posing routines. This was the opening scene from *Pumping Iron,* a behind-the-scenes look at bodybuilding. The film focused on several bodybuilders, including Schwarzenegger, Columbu, and Lou Ferrigno (who would go on to star in the television show *The Incredible Hulk*). While the movie illustrated the sheer will and dedication involved in training, it also put a human face on each bodybuilder. These men had hopes, fears, ambitions, and a sense of humor.

Schwarzenegger emerged as the clear star of *Pumping Iron*. Viewers saw him earnestly confiding to the camera and joking around with his training buddies. When the movie came out in 1977, even the toughest critics had to admit that Schwarzenegger had an appealing presence.

By this time, Schwarzenegger was making a small fortune from his business deals. He bought a house in Santa Monica, started driving a Mercedes, and began dressing more fashionably. Schwarzenegger vowed to continue promoting bodybuilding and had even formed a business partnership with bodybuilding promoter Jim Lorimer. Together, they established an annual competition in Columbus, Ohio, that became known as the Arnold Classic. At the same time, Schwarzenegger promoted himself. Along with Douglas Kent Hall, he wrote his autobiography, *Arnold: The Education of a Bodybuilder*. The book included Schwarzenegger's tips and exercises for fitness fans, and it became a best-seller. In the coming years, he would write several popular fitness books for men, women, and children.

MEETING MARIA

Schwarzenegger's new celebrity status earned him invitations to star-studded events. In August 1977, he was invited to the Robert F. Kennedy Tennis Tournament in Forest Hills, New York. At the tournament, Schwarzenegger was introduced to Maria Shriver, a

Schwarzenegger and Maria at dinner with friends in August 1978

member of the younger generation of Kennedys, one
of the country's premier political families. Maria was
the daughter of Eunice Kennedy Shriver and a niece
of assassinated U.S. president John F. Kennedy. Maria
and Schwarzenegger hit it off immediately. Before he
knew it, he was boarding a plane for Hyannis Port on
Cape Cod, Massachusetts, to spend the weekend at the
Kennedy family home.

Known for their liberal views on social issues, the
Kennedys and Shrivers are staunch Democrats.
Schwarzenegger's political ideas were closer to those
of the Republican Party. But he was comfortable with
the Kennedy family immediately, despite their political differences. He was soon spending a great deal of
time with them. He conversed in German with Maria's
father, Sargent Shriver, a businessman and politician.
Schwarzenegger also chatted in German with Rose
Kennedy, Maria's grandmother, as they took long
walks together.

In the time he spent with the Kennedys and Shrivers, Schwarzenegger discovered the value of public service. Schwarzenegger later recalled something Sargent Shriver said: "Break that mirror in front of you—that mirror that only lets you look at yourself. Break it, so you look beyond! You'll see the rest of the world. You'll see the people who need your help!"

Maria's mother, Eunice Kennedy Shriver, introduced Schwarzenegger to the Special Olympics, an organization she had founded to provide athletic training and sports competitions to people with mental disabilities. Schwarzenegger agreed to serve as the honorary weightlifting coach for the Special Olympics. He traveled around the country, giving weight lifting demonstrations and raising money for Special Olympics programs.

Schwarzenegger and Maria's romance developed. Maria has claimed it was love at first sight, while Schwarzenegger said he grew to love her more each time he saw her. Maria seemed like Schwarzenegger's perfect match—intelligent, confident, and tough. But their early relationship was tested by distance. Eight years younger than the thirty-year-old Schwarzenegger, Maria had just graduated from Georgetown University when they met. She was eager to start a career in journalism. A television station in Philadelphia, Pennsylvania, hired her as a writer and producer, and she stayed there a year before moving to a similar job in Baltimore, Maryland.

SPECIAL OLYMPICS

et me win. But if I cannot win, let me be brave in the attempt.

—The Special Olympics oath

A roaring crowd fills the stadium, cheering as athletes from around the world parade behind the flags of their countries. Many of the athletes have spent years training for this moment—the opening ceremonies of the International Special Olympic Games. In the days ahead, they will compete in events ranging from cycling to powerlifting to volleyball. What makes these athletes special is that they have mental disabilities that can make participating in sports an extra challenge. Through the Special Olympics program, however, they have gained self-confidence and improved their physical fitness.

The story of the Special Olympics dates to the early 1960s, when Eunice Kennedy Shriver started a day camp for people who are mentally disabled. When she saw how enthusiastic and capable the campers were when it came to sports, the idea for the Special Olympics was born. Since 1968, when the first International Special Olympics Games were held in Chicago, Illinois, millions of children and adults with mental disabilities have taken part in the program.

These days athletes from all fifty states and more than 150 nations train and compete in twenty-six different sports. They work with more than 500,000 volunteers—including Schwarzenegger, who became the International Weight Training Coach in 1979. He travels the world to spread the news about Special Olympics, with the goal of increasing acceptance and equal opportunity for the mentally disabled. "I've met countless athletes and families who wage a daily battle against the incredible odds stacked against them," said Schwarzenegger. "Overcoming obstacles is a way of life for them—and an inspiration for me."

Schwarzenegger visited Maria as often as possible, but he was also focused on his acting career in California. In 1978 he appeared in *The Villain,* a western spoof for which he earned $275,000. The critics trashed everything about the movie except Schwarzenegger's performance. Schwarzenegger made a cameo appearance in 1979 in an unsuccessful comedy called *Scavenger Hunt.* That same year, he served as an expert commentator for the CBS telecast of the Mr. Olympia contest. A wider television audience watched him in CBS's *The Jayne Mansfield Story,* in which he played bodybuilder Mickey Hargitay opposite Loni Anderson as movie actress Jayne Mansfield. Schwarzenegger's delightful and sensitive performance earned him high praise from the critics.

A RISING STAR

Schwarzenegger continued to search for just the right role in a movie with box-office potential, a part that would put him in demand as an actor. In 1980 director John Milius was casting *Conan the Barbarian,* a fantasy epic about a slave turned fearless warrior. Milius believed Schwarzenegger, the owner of the world's best body, was the only man to play the title role. Schwarzenegger knew this was his big chance. In the months before the movie went into production, he trained hard at the gym, took acting classes, studied martial arts, and learned to fight with a sword. The filming of *Conan the Barbarian* was grueling, and

In Conan the Barbarian, *Schwarzenegger plays a man who had been sold into slavery as a boy after his parents were killed. When he grows up, he seeks revenge for his parents' deaths.*

Schwarzenegger suffered several painful injuries. But he was thrilled. For the first time, he was the star of a major motion picture.

Schwarzenegger was in such good shape by the time the 1980 Mr. Olympia competition rolled around that he decided to come out of retirement and enter. When he won, he created a furor among some body-builders, who claimed the judges showed favoritism. Others said Schwarzenegger deserved to win and had psyched out his opponents with his surprise entry.

Life was busy for Schwarzenegger and Maria. When *Conan the Barbarian* hit the movie theaters in 1982, it was an instant success. Schwarzenegger was a star. At the same time, Maria was becoming a standout in the world of television news. She was living in California and working as a reporter. In 1983 she landed the

Arnold Schwarzenegger in
The Terminator

position of West Coast reporter for the *CBS Morning News,* a network job with a national audience. That same year, on September 16, Schwarzenegger marked another high point in his life. Holding a small American flag, he took the oath that made him an American citizen. Schwarzenegger now held dual citizenship, both Austrian and American.

After starring in a successful sequel to *Conan the Barbarian,* called *Conan the Destroyer,* Schwarzenegger catapulted to further fame in his next film, *The Terminator.* He played a cyborg—part man, part machine—who time-travels from the year 2029 to 1984 Los Angeles. The Terminator's mission is to change the future by changing the past. The Terminator must find and kill a woman named Sarah Connor, whose unborn son will lead humans to victory over cyborgs in a future war.

In *The Terminator,* Schwarzenegger played an emotionless machine, bent only on finding Sarah Connor. He had very few lines, but one would become a classic movie quote. After trying unsuccessfully to capture

Sarah at a police station, the Terminator, with a thick Austrian accent, tells the desk sergeant, "I'll be back!" Soon, even people who hadn't seen the movie were repeating the phrase.

The Terminator received top marks from critics. Some thought it was one of the best films of 1984. The movie broke new ground in science fiction films, proving to be both intelligent and filled with action-packed adventure. And it sealed Schwarzenegger's future as an action-adventure movie star. "With *The Terminator,*" Schwarzenegger later said, "I think people became aware of the fact that I did not really have to take my shirt off or run around and expose my muscles in order to sell tickets."

WEDDING BELLS

In 1985, after roles in the dismal *Red Sonja* and the much more successful *Commando,* Schwarzenegger took Maria on a trip to Austria. As he showed her around his old haunts in Thal, they came to the lake where Schwarzenegger had played with his friends as a boy. Maria suggested they take a rowboat out on the water. There, surrounded by the lush greenery of summer and the sound of lapping water, Schwarzenegger proposed to Maria. On August 10, 1985, they announced their engagement to the world.

Three weeks later, CBS offered Maria a shot at the big time, the opportunity to coanchor the *CBS Morning News* alongside Forrest Sawyer. But it would mean going to New York and wrestling with a long-distance relationship again. Schwarzenegger encouraged Maria to go after her career goals. She took the job in New York and traveled home to California on weekends to see Schwarzenegger. As he started work on the movie *Raw Deal* that fall, the couple made wedding plans.

At about 10:00 A.M. on April 26, 1986, limousines and rented buses began arriving at the Church of St. Francis Xavier in Hyannis Port. Reporters, photographers, and excited fans—some of whom had climbed trees to get a better view—watched the guests gathering for Schwarzenegger and Maria's wedding. A few Hollywood celebrities were invited, but Schwarzenegger and Maria planned to spend the day surrounded by family members and close friends. The Kennedy and Shriver clans arrived, including maid of honor Caroline Kennedy, John F. Kennedy's daughter. Aurelia, who had hosted an Austrian-themed rehearsal dinner the previous evening, entered the church smiling warmly. Schwarzenegger ducked in a back door and met up with his best man, Franco Columbu, while Maria arrived in a beautiful white gown with an eleven-foot train.

After the priest pronounced them husband and wife, Schwarzenegger and Maria were whisked away to their reception, where guests feasted on a lunch of lobster, oysters, and chicken, followed by a towering wedding cake weighing 425 pounds. The couple spent the afternoon dancing and accepting the warm wishes of their guests. The revelry stopped for only a few moments

Schwarzenegger is all smiles as he presents his new wife, Maria Shriver, after their wedding on April 26, 1986.

when Schwarzenegger presented his new in-laws with a painting of Maria done by wedding guest and famous artist Andy Warhol. "I'm not really taking her away," Schwarzenegger told Maria's parents, "because I am giving this to you so you will always have her. I love her and I will always take care of her."

After their wedding, Schwarzenegger and Maria took up residence in their new Pacific Palisades, California, mansion. The Spanish-style home, set among gardens, had seven bedrooms, four bathrooms, a swimming pool, tennis courts, and a gym. Schwarzenegger immediately returned to shooting the movie *Predator,* which he had been working on in Mexico before the wedding. Maria's CBS show was canceled in September, but she soon landed another position with NBC. Life was good for Schwarzenegger and Maria, and it would only get better.

Arnold Schwarzenegger starred in Predator *in 1987.*

Chapter **FIVE**

FAME, FORTUNE, AND POLITICS

BY THE LATE **1980**S, SCHWARZENEGGER WAS A box-office megastar, acclaimed for his powerful screen presence. He had found his niche in action-adventure films and was making hit after hit. In 1987 Schwarzenegger received the 1,847th star on the Hollywood Walk of Fame. That same year *Predator,* a frightening movie about a military unit stalked by an alien, was released. It was followed by the science fiction thriller *The Running Man* and then *Red Heat,* the first film that brought Schwarzenegger a $10 million paycheck. Schwarzenegger controlled his career, actively promoting himself the same way a company would promote a product. He eagerly traveled the world to do publicity for his movies—something many other big stars are unwilling to do. "I'm a business-man," said Schwarzenegger. "I'm interested in the movie making money. I'm not hung up on being an actor's actor or doing what they call artistic movies."

Although Schwarzenegger would always identify himself with the action-adventure genre, he thought it was time for a new challenge. He had been longing to stretch his acting muscles and star in a comedy. "You have to give your fans what they expect," he said. "But then you slowly add on. You give them a little bit of something else, something new. You put a little more clothes on in each movie and show another side of you—more humor, or more sensitivity. Eventually, I'll do a movie that's entirely comedy." But movie executives did not see comedies in Schwarzenegger's future. Because they weren't sending him scripts, Schwarzenegger made it happen himself.

The 1988 movie *Twins* was written specifically for Schwarzenegger. He stars as Julius Benedict, the product of a scientific experiment that gave him six genetically superior fathers. Julius discovers that his mother also gave birth to his twin brother, who due to his lack of superior breeding was sent to an orphanage. Julius goes in search of his brother, finds him in jail, and bails him out. Julius's twin is Vincent, a short and pushy hustler played by Danny DeVito. Julius convinces Vincent that they should look for their long-lost mother, and the twins set out on their misadventures. The visual image of Schwarzenegger

In the movie Twins, Schwarzenegger's character meets his twin brother, played by actor Danny DeVito (left), and they go in search of their mother. In the film, Schwarzenegger proved he could act in comedies as well as action-adventure movies.

and DeVito as twin brothers was amusing enough, but it turned out that Schwarzenegger was the perfect straight man for the funny DeVito. The movie was a hit with both audiences and critics, and it proved that Schwarzenegger had range as an actor.

THE GOOD LIFE

Three years into their marriage, Schwarzenegger and Maria had settled into a comfortable life. Their house held Schwarzenegger's beloved art collection—including a Chagall, a Miró, and a full-length portrait of him by LeRoy Neiman. His boyhood dream car, a 1957 Cadillac, as well as a Harley-Davidson motorcycle, were parked in the garage. When he was not filming a movie, he spent free time at home, working out, playing tennis, or riding his motorcycle. Sometimes he and Maria went horseback riding or relaxed and

Schwarzenegger poses in a 1950s Cadillac convertible.

watched movies. In the evenings, he often worked
late, pouring over scripts and asking Maria for advice
on the nights she was home from New York. "Maria
has very good instincts," Schwarzenegger said. "She
reads fast, she analyzes and—boom!—she has the
notes. Like an agent."

The couple decided that the time was right to start a
family. In December 1989, their first child, Katherine
Eunice, was born. At first, Maria tried to continue the
hectic pace of her East Coast job. But she soon realized that it was not going to work with a baby at
home. Disappointed, she gave up her anchor job and
began working part-time for NBC in Los Angeles. But
this mix of work and family turned out to be a great

balance for Maria. Over the coming years, their family grew to include a second daughter, Christina Aurelia, and sons Patrick Arnold and Christopher Sargent. Schwarzenegger became a family man first and foremost, always staying involved with his children.

Schwarzenegger's growing real estate holdings and other business deals also kept him busy. He was a wheeler-dealer who made smart investments. One was a $10 million venture called Main Street Plaza in Santa Monica, where he established the offices of his company, Oak Productions. He and Maria also opened a restaurant there called Schatzi on Main. The restaurant's menu offers some of Schwarzenegger's favorite

Schwarzenegger opened a restaurant called Schatzi on Main in Santa Monica. Schatzi means "sweetheart" in German.

Business partners and movie stars Schwarzenegger and Bruce Willis (right) attend the opening of a Planet Hollywood in Las Vegas, Nevada.

Austrian foods and features apple strudel made from his mother's recipe.

Schwarzenegger did face one much-publicized business failure. He and other Hollywood actors, including Sylvester Stallone and Bruce Willis, invested in a worldwide chain of restaurants. Called Planet Hollywood, the restaurants featured movie memorabilia and dishes named after popular stars. Ninety-five Planet Hollywoods opened with splashy parties, but the eateries lost their popularity in the late 1990s, and Schwarzenegger severed ties with the company.

GETTING PHYSICAL

Throughout his years of success, Schwarzenegger stayed in touch with the world of politics. Still feeling at home in the camp of the conservative and business-minded Republicans, Schwarzenegger attended the 1984 Republican National Convention in Dallas, Texas.

He later campaigned for Vice President George H. W. Bush, who sought and won the presidency in 1988. During a campaign trip through the Midwest, Schwarzenegger and Bush began discussing the importance of physical fitness. In January 1990, President Bush appointed Schwarzenegger the chairman of the President's Council on Physical Fitness.

Schwarzenegger was serious about making a difference in the lives of children throughout the country. He wanted quality physical education classes to be part of the daily routine at every school. To promote this idea, he promised to visit all fifty states to meet with government representatives, school leaders, and students. He was so determined that he bought a private jet,

Schwarzenegger (center, in white T-shirt), **stands on the White House lawn with President George Bush and Barbara Bush** (both to his right) **to promote physical fitness on May 1, 1990.**

hired a pilot, and set off on his mission. He was going to sell physical fitness to the country. To this end, he held press conferences wherever he went, with kids in the background having fun exercising. In meetings, he discussed specific ideas for helping states pay for physical education classes, including teaming up with private funding sources such as insurance companies. In two years, Schwarzenegger accomplished his goal when he visited his fiftieth state—Ohio. Schwarzenegger's ability to rally people to a cause and use the media to his advantage had some people speculating that he would run for public office one day.

Schwarzenegger rallied forces for another cause in the early 1990s, when he helped create the Inner-City Games program in Los Angeles. The group's mission is to involve inner-city youth in sports as well as educational and cultural programs. By helping kids stay busy after school, the program aims to keep them off drugs and out of gangs. Within ten years, the program would expand to fifteen major U.S. cities.

MAKING MOVIES

In the 1990s, Schwarzenegger lit up the screen in a streak of blockbuster movies. The futuristic *Total Recall*, released in 1990, digs into the mind of a man who does not know which is real—his life as a construction worker on Earth or a life on Mars that haunts his dreams. It was the most complex character that Schwarzenegger had played. Critics raved, with some calling it the best performance of Schwarzenegger's career. It was the biggest hit of the summer at the box office and later received a special Academy Award for its spectacular visual effects.

Schwarzenegger switched gears in his next movie, the 1990 comedy *Kindergarten Cop*. He played a detective named John Kimble who goes undercover as a kindergarten teacher to find the son of a wanted drug dealer. Kimble dives into his undercover assignment with no experience in taking care of a classroom full of children. "They're six-year-olds," he says. "How much trouble can they be?" Again, Schwarzenegger scored a critical and box-office hit. He proved that *Twins* was not a fluke—he could be a bankable star in both action-adventure and comedy films.

In 1991 Schwarzenegger was back in the role of the Terminator in *Terminator 2: Judgment Day*. The Terminator again produced a classic movie quote: "Hasta la vista, baby!" *Terminator 2* rocketed to the top of the box-office charts when it opened in July. But Schwarzenegger hit a rough spot in his next film, 1993's *Last Action Hero*. Critics gave it mixed reviews, and theater attendance trailed off after the first week. Schwarzenegger returned to the successful formula of combining comedy and adventure for *True Lies,* released in 1994. Schwarzenegger played Harry Tasker, a government agent so deep undercover that he can't tell his wife, Helen, what he does for a living. Helen, played by Jamie Lee Curtis, believes he's a

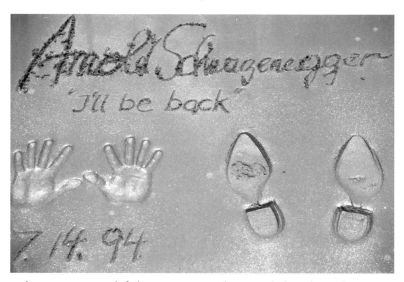

Schwarzenegger left his signature along with hand- and footprints in the sidewalk cement outside Grauman's Chinese Theater in Hollywood.

computer salesman. When Tasker is set on the trail of a nuclear terrorist, Helen thinks he's having an affair. The movie's humorous misunderstandings and fast-paced action appealed to a broad audience. In 1996 Schwarzenegger starred in *Eraser* as U.S. marshal John Kruger. Kruger's job was to erase the memories of people in the government's witness relocation program.

In 1997 both Maria and Schwarzenegger suffered health problems. Maria had a difficult fourth pregnancy and had to be hospitalized. Schwarzenegger, at age forty-nine, underwent heart surgery to replace an aortic valve that had been damaged since birth.

FAMILY DEATHS

The Schwarzeneggers mourned the loss of some close family members in the 1990s. Maria's grandmother, Rose Kennedy, died in 1995 at the age of 104. In 1998 Schwarzenegger's mother passed away at age 76, and Maria's cousin Michael Kennedy died in a skiing accident. In 1999 her cousin John F. Kennedy Jr. and his wife, Carolyn Bessette, were killed in a private plane crash off the coast of Massachusetts, while en route to a Kennedy family wedding.

"I've never felt sick or had any symptoms at all, but I knew I'd have to take care of this condition sooner or later," Schwarzenegger stated. "I said to the doctors, 'Let's do it now while I'm young and healthy.'"

Quickly recovering, Schwarzenegger continued to make action-adventure movies and comedies. *The 6th Day* and *Collateral Damage* were successful. But *Jingle All the Way, Batman & Robin,* and *End of Days* did not draw the expected theater crowds. Some critics suggested that Schwarzenegger was losing his touch at the box office.

FAMILY AND POLITICS

Schwarzenegger and Maria both found great joy in raising their children. With two successful careers, they became a very wealthy couple. But they tried to make

*Schwarzenegger, Maria, and their kids took a family trip to
South Africa in July 2001. Despite their busy careers,
Schwarzenegger and Maria make family life a priority.*

life as normal as possible for their kids, assigning them
chores, restricting phone and television privileges,
checking their homework, and having family dinners.

While Schwarzenegger's movie schedule eased in the
new century, his interest in politics grew. He even considered running for governor of California in 2002. But
he was committed to *Terminator 3: Rise of the Machines*
for a record-breaking salary of $30 million. He returned
to a strict training regimen to get back into his buff
Terminator physique. And when filming began, he
focused all his energy on making it a great film.

Although his work on *Terminator 3* did not allow time for an election campaign, Schwarzenegger did throw himself into a cause he firmly believed in—after-school programs. On the November 2002 ballot, California voters would decide whether or not to fund the After School Education and Safety Act (Proposition 49), an initiative led by Schwarzenegger. "One million kids under the age of fifteen are home alone after school," Schwarzenegger explained. "These are kids that do not have anyone to do homework with them, take them to the sport field, or hug them." The initiative passed, and $550 million dollars was earmarked for after-school programs.

As Schwarzenegger set out to promote *Terminator 3,* a movement was under way to unseat Democratic governor Gray Davis. Speculation was building that Schwarzenegger would run for election. He downplayed the rumors, but at the same time dropped some interesting hints. In one case, he said, "Making movies to me now is how bodybuilding felt in 1973 or 1974, when I kept contemplating retiring every year. . . . So now I feel like that with the movie business, that I'm looking forward to a change. It's now not just about my career or about me but about helping millions and millions of people. Imagine the joy in that. Imagine how intense you can get about that."

Schwarzenegger smiles on the set of The Tonight Show *with Jay Leno on August 6, 2003.*

Chapter **SIX**

GOVERNOR
SCHWARZENEGGER

ON THE AFTERNOON OF AUGUST 6, 2003,
hundreds of people formed a line that snaked around
NBC Studios in Burbank, California. Inside, more
than fifty reporters from around the world crowded
into a pressroom. They were all there to see Arnold
Schwarzenegger make an announcement on *The
Tonight Show*. As host Jay Leno cracked jokes during
his monologue, the anticipation was building. Would
Schwarzenegger declare that he was running for governor of California in the upcoming recall election?

All indications were that the answer would be no. In
recent days, Schwarzenegger had consulted with political advisers. And most importantly, he had consulted
with Maria. Coming from a political family, she

understood the difficulties and the sacrifices their family would have to make. Reportedly, she was against Schwarzenegger making a run for governor, and he wouldn't do it without her complete support. His movie career was also at issue. If he won, he would have to put acting on hold and abandon some lucrative business deals. He was not going to run, his advisers were convinced, as they stood by for Schwarzenegger's official announcement.

Leno introduced Schwarzenegger, who sauntered on stage looking calm and cool in a crisp white shirt and black suit. He was all smiles as he settled in to talk with the host. When Leno broached the subject of the recall election, Schwarzenegger began to speak his mind. "The politicians are fiddling, fumbling, and failing," he said. "The man that is failing the people more than anyone is Gray Davis. He is failing them terribly, and this is why he needs to be recalled. And this is why I am going to run for governor."

The studio audience erupted in cheers, and Leno shook his head in amazement. Schwarzenegger's political advisers were stunned, still holding their copies of the prepared statement that said he would not be running. In the pressroom, even reporters were shocked into silence—for a moment, at least—before grabbing their cell phones to call the news in to their editors. Schwarzenegger had scripted his announcement perfectly, bringing all the drama and suspense of his action-adventure movies to the political arena.

On national television, Schwarzenegger discussed his plans to run for California governor with Jay Leno.

In the pressroom after the show, Schwarzenegger talked about the difficult decision to run for governor. Throughout his promotional tour for *Terminator 3*, he had thought about it and discussed it with Maria and their children. Maria had seen how passionate Schwarzenegger was about the issues facing California and finally threw her support behind him. The choice was his. Schwarzenegger felt it was his duty to run. He said he knew the problems the state faced and that he had the persistence and know-how to tackle them.

On the street outside, a crowd had gathered after hearing the news. A cry of "Aaaahhhnold!" went up as Schwarzenegger, followed closely by cameras and reporters, set off to meet the voters. With promises to "pump up" the state government and say "hasta la vista, baby" to the bad politicians, Schwarzenegger the candidate set off to conquer California politics.

A PETITION FOR CHANGE

California has a reputation among the other forty-nine states as being a bit wacky. But recalling Gray Davis, a Democratic governor who had been elected to a second term less than a year before, was beyond wacky to many people. Political pundits dubbed the election "a freak show," "a train wreck," and "democracy run amok." But other political experts said Californians were simply asserting their rights by following the recall provision that has been in the state's constitution since 1911. And Californians certainly hadn't abused this power. In fact, the statewide recall election would be the first in California's history.

So how did Californians become so frustrated with their governor that they wanted to dismiss him from office? The driving issue was the condition of the state's economy. During the 1990s, Internet businesses were booming in California. The state government collected a lot of money from these companies through taxes, and by 1998 there was a budget surplus of $12 billion, meaning that the government had much more money than it needed to run the state. But many Internet companies were financially unstable, and by 2000, most had gone out of business. They no longer supplied the state with huge tax revenues, but the budget for the huge state of California needed large amounts of money to continue functioning. By the time Davis came up for reelection in 2002, the state had a budget deficit—the government needed more money to run the state than it actually had to spend. California was not the only state in this situation. Much of the country was suffering through an economic downturn. Davis assured Californians that the state's budget problems were mild and could be managed. With this in mind, voters stayed the course and elected Davis to a second term, expecting that he would lead the state through its economic woes.

After the election, the extent of California's budget crisis became apparent. By the spring of 2003, the deficit had grown to $35 billion dollars—the biggest shortfall in the state's history—and it was growing by millions of dollars every day. Many Californians felt Davis had lied to them during the election. They accused him of downplaying the state's financial problems to win reelection. Davis's solution to balancing the budget—raising taxes—further angered the public. The governor's approval rating plunged to 21 percent, and a poll found that only 9 percent of voters had confidence in Davis's ability to fix the state's problems. Gray Davis was the most unpopular governor in California history.

The idea of recalling Davis took root. The step was drastic but necessary, some said, to save the state from financial ruin. U.S. Representative Darrell Issa,

During California's debate on whether to recall elected governor Gray Davis (left), many Democrats spoke on Davis's behalf. Here General Wesley Clark (right), then a presidential nominee hopeful, speaks to a crowd.

a Republican, started and helped fund an expensive recall effort called "Rescue California." Issa's goal was to gather the 897,158 signatures needed on a petition to recall Davis. (That number equaled 12 percent of the number of votes cast in the previous California election for governor.) By July 2003, the petition had more than 1.3 million valid signatures, and the recall election was set to take place October 7.

Davis said that he understood that Californians were frustrated over the state's budget problems. But he labeled the recall effort "a hostile takeover" by Republicans and promised he would "fight like a Bengal tiger." Issa countered by saying, "If you create a problem, lie about a problem, and have no fix for a problem, it's time for you to go as soon as possible."

The October 7 ballot would ask voters two questions. First, should Gray Davis be recalled as governor of

California? Second, if he is recalled, who should be the next governor?

CANDIDATE SCHWARZENEGGER

When Schwarzenegger announced his candidacy for governor, his fame as an actor made him an immediate front-runner for the position. Before long, people began comparing him to other actors and celebrities who had entered politics. The most frequent yardstick they measured him against was Ronald Reagan, an actor who became governor of California in 1966 and served as president of the United States from 1981 to 1989. Both men entered a race for political office at about the same age—Schwarzenegger at fifty-six and Reagan at fifty-five. They share rugged good looks and a toughness of character. Both have charisma and a certain ease in relating to a crowd. And they are both Republicans. Schwarzenegger greatly admires Reagan and keeps a bust of him in his office. Lyn Nofziger, who once worked as a political adviser to Reagan, suggested that the former president blazed a trail for Schwarzenegger. "When Reagan got into politics, running for governor, it was fashionable to say he was just a dumb actor mouthing lines he had memorized that someone put in his mouth and he was not really competent to get up there and speak on his feet," said Nofziger. "He proved that being an actor is not necessarily a negative."

Schwarzenegger's run for governor also reminded people of his friend Jesse Ventura, a professional wrestler and actor who had appeared with Schwarzenegger in *Predator*. The flashy and straight-talking Ventura shocked the political world when he was elected governor of Minnesota in 1998. He became the first member of the Reform Party to win a major office, making him an outsider in America's two-party political system. Because of his show business background, people hadn't taken him seriously as a candidate. Some people dismissed Schwarzenegger's candidacy the same way, wondering how Californians could seriously consider voting for the action-adventure movie star.

Although Schwarzenegger had the strength of his Republican affiliation behind him, he had few political connections in California. He was a celebrity, not a political insider. But like Ventura, Schwarzenegger turned his lack of political experience into an asset. He was different from all the career politicians, he pointed out. He did not owe anyone any political favors. Schwarzenegger promised that he was a man of action who would do what was best for California. Ventura had rallied young voters who did not have a good record of going to the polls. Schwarzenegger would work to do the same with his young movie fans.

Like Reagan and Ventura, Schwarzenegger considers himself a fiscal conservative. He strongly believes in keeping taxes low so that money stays in the pockets of the people and businesses that earn it. Unlike many

Eager kids from the Inner-City Games Foundation get to talk with Schwarzenegger, who helped create the organization.

Republicans, Schwarzenegger is more moderate in his views on social issues. He supports gun control, abortion rights, gay rights, and protection of the environment. Some people attribute his stance on these issues to his relationship with his wife and her family, who have a long history of liberalism. Maria's father started the Peace Corps, and her brothers work for such organizations as the Special Olympics, Save the Children, and the mentoring program Best Buddies. Schwarzenegger's own work in American schools probably shaped some of his opinions on education and other social issues.

Although Schwarzenegger has great respect for the Shriver and Kennedy legacy, he has always stood firmly in the Republican camp. He would do things his way and did not expect any public support from his wife's family during the campaign. Ted Kennedy, Maria's uncle and a Democratic senator from Massachusetts, told reporters "I like and respect Arnold, and I've been impressed with his efforts to promote after-school education in California and his willingness to come to Congress and the administration to fight for that program. But I'm a Democrat and I don't support the recall effort." On a personal level, however, the Kennedys and Shrivers wished Schwarzenegger well, as they would any member of their family.

In California, voters saw in Schwarzenegger a self-made man and a tough business manager who could help solve California's financial crisis. At the same time, they saw someone who understood the hardships and challenges many in the state face every day. Like millions of Californians, Schwarzenegger was an immigrant who had arrived in the United States with almost nothing. Yet he was living the American Dream. He told voters that he wanted to repay the state he loved for all it had given him. "You have such a fantastic life, Arnold. You make millions of dollars to do movies and all those kinds of things. Why do you want to do this?" Schwarzenegger said he asked himself. "And you know something, because everything that I've gotten—my career, my money, my family—everything I've gotten and achieved is because of California."

On the Campaign Trail

The day after announcing his intentions on *The Tonight Show,* Schwarzenegger made his way through an admiring crowd of office workers in the Los Angeles County government building to officially file his candidacy for governor. When the ballot was printed, Schwarzenegger's name would be listed among 135 candidates from all walks of life, representing eight political parties. The candidates were businesspeople, lawyers, teachers, college students, and firefighters. There was a railroad worker, a doctor, a former baseball commissioner, and even a sumo wrestler. And

Arnold Schwarzenegger speaks to the press outside the Los Angeles County Registrar's Office after filing his paperwork to run for California governor.

there were other entertainers, including 1980s TV star Gary Coleman and the comedian Gallagher. Besides Gray Davis, Schwarzenegger's most serious opponents would be Republican state senator Tom McClintock and Democratic lieutenant governor Cruz Busta-mante—who, in support of his party, urged people to vote no for the recall and yes for him.

Schwarzenegger's surprise announcement left his advisers scrambling to set up a campaign office. With only sixty-two days to campaign, they had to hit the ground running. One thing they did not have to worry about was name recognition. Everyone knew who Schwarzenegger was, and he was mobbed wherever he went. Crowd control and security became a big issue. Campaign staffers began scheduling campaign stops based on how many bicycle racks were on site. Used as barriers, the metal racks were tall enough to keep the crowd back but low enough for Schwarzenegger to reach across to shake voters' hands. Not all the people lined up to see him were fans, however. In one incident during a stop in Long Beach, California, someone in the crowd pelted Schwarzenegger with eggs. But he barely broke his stride. He just took off his jacket and laughed, saying, "This guy owes me bacon now."

A lack of organization and some missteps in the first few weeks of the campaign moved Schwarzenegger down in the polls. He had added prestigious investor and billionaire Warren Buffett to his team as an economic adviser. But the campaign pushed Buffett into the background after he was quoted as saying California's property taxes were too low—not something the state's residents wanted to hear. Then it came out that Schwarzenegger had once supported a controversial 1994 measure called Proposition 187 that would deny public services to illegal immigrants. Some voters began to doubt that Schwarzenegger was the right choice for California.

When Schwarzenegger hit the campaign trail in earnest, he began portraying himself as the "governor for the people." He was the outsider, someone people could trust to make decisions for them. Schwarzenegger stood for change, his campaign said, while Davis

Schwarzenegger pumps up a crowd on the campaign trail.

and Bustamante represented failed policies that had not worked. During campaign stops, Schwarzenegger was good at firing up a crowd. He used lines from his movies and pop culture, saying he would "terminate" business as usual in Sacramento (the state's capital) or that it was "game over" for Governor Davis.

It was not clear, however, what Schwarzenegger planned to do exactly to fix California. The press began asking him tough policy questions, ones he hadn't had time to figure out yet. His lack of political experience began to show. But soon his campaign staff was pulling together detailed position statements and releasing them to the press. News reports indicated that Schwarzenegger was finally getting down to business. He participated in only one of three debates, on September 24, at which he stuck to one-liners and generalities. But one debate was enough to solidify support for Schwarzenegger among voters. In the polls, he moved from a tie with Bustamante into the lead.

Schwarzenegger took advantage of his celebrity status during the campaign to reach a broad audience. He granted an interview to the celebrity news show *Access Hollywood*. His face beamed from the covers of *Time* and *Newsweek*, and he was featured in one-on-one news interviews with ABC's Peter Jennings and NBC's Tom Brokaw. He appeared on other national television shows, including *Oprah* and *Larry King Live*. For her show, Oprah Winfrey—a longtime friend of Maria's—interviewed Schwarzenegger and Maria together, giving voters in California and people across the country a look at Schwarzenegger the family man. Schwarzenegger and Maria talked about their children and the values that are important to them. Actor Rob Lowe signed on to Schwarzenegger's campaign team to rally support among other celebrities. Comedian Dana Carvey, who had regularly spoofed Schwarzenegger on the comedy show *Saturday Night Live,* made an appearance, imitating Schwarzenegger's accent and highlighting the candidate's sense of humor.

Schwarzenegger's colorful and energetic campaign contrasted sharply with those of his opponents. Davis, Bustamante, and McClintock all seemed dull in comparison and reminded many voters of politics as usual. While Schwarzenegger took a moderate position and reached out to people of all parties, Davis and Bustamante stuck to rallying Democrats. And McClintock appealed to conservative Republicans. Some members of the Republican Party suggested that McClintock should bow out of the race to prevent splitting the Republican vote. But he refused, saying he was in it to the finish line. Davis brought in the big guns from the Democratic Party to campaign for him, including former president Bill Clinton and several of the candidates running in the 2004 presidential election. Throughout the campaign, he positioned himself as a victim of an unfair recall process rather than tackling other issues. In the meantime, Schwarzenegger focused on comparing himself to Davis and Bustamante.

By the end of September 2003, it looked like the election belonged to Schwarzenegger. Confident that victory was at hand, Schwarzenegger laid out a plan for his first 100 days as governor. At a rally in San Francisco on October 1, he told about four hundred supporters, "We are ready to take office. We are ready to take action. We are ready to return California to the people." His first move would be to repeal a recent and very unpopular tax increase that had tripled vehicle registration fees. Other immediate plans included having the state budget audited, calling a special session of the legislature to determine spending cuts, and renegotiating state employee union contracts—all issues that resonated with voters.

"PUKE POLITICS"

The day Schwarzenegger had announced his candidacy, he told reporters, "I know they're going to throw everything at me and they're going to say... that I'm a womanizer, that I'm a terrible guy, and all these kind of things are going to come my way." He was right. Schwarzenegger faced tough accusations throughout his campaign. But the worst of what he called "puke politics" did not come until a few days before the election.

On October 2, five days before voters were due to go to the polls, the *Los Angeles Times* published a story alleging that Schwarzenegger had sexually harassed several women. In interviews, the women said Schwarzenegger made unwelcome advances, some of which took place on movie sets. The timing of the article drew questions. Why had the *Times* waited until then to break the story? Had Democrats—specifically Gray Davis's campaign—played a role in passing information to the newspaper? The *Times* insisted that it was not playing politics. The paper's duty, the editor said, was to investigate someone who might be California's next governor. Reporters had started working on the story when Schwarzenegger announced his candidacy. It was only now being published because the reporters needed time to find the women, verify their stories, and write the article. Both Davis and the *Times* strongly denied any collaboration.

Schwarzenegger did not deny the sexual harassment allegations, but he did downplay them. "A lot of what you see in the stories is not true," he said. "At the same time, I have to tell you what I always have to say: wherever there is smoke, there is fire." He went on to apologize. "Yes, I have behaved badly sometimes," he said. "Yes, it is true that I was on rowdy movie sets and I have done things that were not right that I thought were playful. I now recognize that I have offended people, and to those people that I offended I want to say that I am deeply sorry and I apologize." He vowed to be a "champion of women" if elected.

Throughout the campaign, Maria had faced questions about her husband's reputation as a womanizer, and she had defended him. In the face of the harassment charges, she stood by him again, saying he showed great courage in apologizing. She rallied support for him among women around the state. "I have been spending the last several weeks engaging remarkable women—Democrats, Republicans, Independents—who are proactive, pro-women, pro-Arnold."

Other accusations plagued Schwarzenegger during the last days of the campaign. A story published in the *New York Times* on October 2 described a book proposal by *Pumping Iron* producer George Butler. Quotes from Schwarzenegger in the book proposal suggested that he admired Nazi leader Adolf Hitler, whose goal was to eliminate all Jews as he tried to conquer the world. Under Hitler's leadership, six

Protesters of the recall and of candidate Schwarzenegger hold up opposition signs at a Schwarzenegger campaign stop.

million Jews were killed in the Holocaust during World War II—more than two-thirds of all the Jews in Europe at that time. Thousands more suffered in Nazi-controlled concentration camps. To be called an admirer of Hitler was a damaging charge.

The New York Times quoted from the book proposal, which said Schwarzenegger admired Hitler because he "came from being a little man with almost no formal education up to power. And I admire him for being such a good public speaker and for his way of getting to the people and so on." A day later, original transcripts of the interview revealed that Schwarzenegger went on to say, "But I did not admire him for what he did with it." Still, the idea that their next governor might be a Nazi sympathizer outraged many voters. During a rally near San Francisco, protesters shouted, "No Nazi for governor" during Schwarzenegger's campaign speech. Schwarzenegger's opponents focused on his character. "I don't see how anyone can admire Adolf Hitler," said Davis. "Any decent American has to be offended by that phrase."

Schwarzenegger firmly denied the charges that he was a Nazi sympathizer. "I think that Hitler was a disgusting villain, dictator, and he has caused so much harm in the world and we have to make sure it never happens again," he said. Schwarzenegger's old friends back in Graz called the accusations ridiculous. In Austria, Schwarzenegger is known as a humanitarian who supports Jewish organizations. In fact, Schwarzenegger raised millions of dollars for the Simon Wiesenthal Center in Los Angeles. The center's founder, Rabbi Marvin Hier, defended Schwarzenegger, noting that he has done more to help the cause of Holocaust awareness than any other movie star.

With all these accusations swirling around him, Schwarzenegger tried to refocus his campaign on the economic problems facing California. With Maria by his side, he set off on a whirlwind tour of the state in a bus with a huge picture of Schwarzenegger's face plastered on the side. The bus was dubbed Running Man, after one of his movies. At rally after rally, he pushed aside the attacks on his character and pumped up the crowds with talk of better leadership and a better future for California. By the weekend before the election, the polls showed him as the clear front-runner.

VICTORY

When the sun rose on October 7, lines were already forming outside California polling places. Voting was steady all day. The election had one of the largest voter turnouts the state had ever seen for a governor's race. When Schwarzenegger and Maria arrived at their polling place in Pacific Palisades, they were greeted by hundreds of reporters and photographers. After Schwarzenegger voted, he joked with the crowd, saying that when his turn came at the voting booth, he had just looked for the longest name on the ten-page ballot.

Schwarzenegger and Maria (left) *step up to the voting booths to cast their ballots during the California recall election on October 7, 2003.*

The polls closed at 8 P.M., and the counting began. Results rolling in clearly indicated that Davis would be recalled and Schwarzenegger would be the next governor of California. In the end, more than 55 percent of voters decided to oust Davis. With nearly 50 percent of the vote, Schwarzenegger topped the list for Davis's replacement, followed by Bustamante with just over 30 percent. The vote was not even close. Schwarzenegger had done just what he intended to do—terminate the competition.

That night, Davis called Schwarzenegger to congratulate him. Both men promised to work hard to make the

After learning of his victory in the recall election on October 7, 2003, Schwarzenegger thanked his family and supporters and acknowledged the hard work that lay ahead

change in leadership a smooth transition. Soon after the call, Davis appeared before his supporters to concede the race and thank them for standing by him throughout his career. "We've had a lot of good nights over the last twenty years, but tonight the people did decide that it's time for someone else to serve, and I accept their judgment," Davis said. Davis became the first governor to be ejected from office since 1921, when North Dakota residents recalled Governor Lynn Frazier.

Schwarzenegger ended his campaign just as he had started it—with an introduction from Jay Leno. Surrounded by family members, friends, and campaign workers, Schwarzenegger began his victory speech by thanking Maria. "I want to thank her so much for being the greatest wife and the most spectacular partner. And I know how many votes I got today because of [her]," he said. There were other thank-yous—to his children and his campaign staff—but he saved his highest praise for Californians. "Today, California has given me the greatest gift of all. You've given me your trust by voting for me," he said. Schwarzenegger went on to talk about the tough job ahead, saying he would reach out to all people to help rebuild California. "Tonight, we are all here celebrating," he said. "But tomorrow, the hard work will begin."

Hard work, ambition, and a great sense of purpose are the driving forces behind Schwarzenegger's success. As a young man, he told friends of his grand goals: to be the best bodybuilder, to become a big movie star, to marry a beautiful and intelligent woman, to be rich, and to be powerful. Having achieved all he ever wanted, he has set new goals and is facing what might be his greatest challenge of all—the role of governor of California, the nation's most populous state.

FILMOGRAPHY

Hercules in New York (1970)
The Long Goodbye (1973)
Stay Hungry (1976)
Pumping Iron (1977)
The Villain (1979)
Scavenger Hunt (1979)
The Comeback (1980)
Conan the Barbarian (1982)
Conan the Destroyer (1984)
The Terminator (1984)
Red Sonja (1985)
Commando (1985)
Raw Deal (1986)
Predator (1987)
The Running Man (1987)
Red Heat (1988)

Twins (1988)
Total Recall (1990)
Kindergarten Cop (1990)
Terminator 2: Judgment Day (1991)
Last Action Hero (1993)
True Lies (1994)
Junior (1994)
Eraser (1996)
Jingle All the Way (1996)
Batman & Robin (1997)
End of Days (1999)
The 6th Day (2000)
Collateral Damage (2002)
Terminator 3: Rise of the Machines (2003)

SOURCES

8   "Schwarzenegger Campaign Releases Two New TV Ads; Focuses on Education, Budget," *PoliticsUS.com,* September 3, 2003, <http://www.politicsus.com /gubernatorial%20press%20releases/Schwarzenegger /090303.htm> (March 2004).

9   "Schwarzenegger: I Will Not Fail You," *CNN.com,* October 8, 2003, <http://edition.cnn.com/2003/ALLPOLITICS /10/08/schwarzenegger.speech/index.html> (March 2004).

15   Arnold Schwarzenegger and Douglas Kent Hall, *Arnold: The Education of a Bodybuilder* (New York: Fireside, 1977), 16.

18   Nigel Andrews, *True Myths: The Life and Times of Arnold Schwarzenegger* (Secaucus, NJ: Birch Lane Press, 1977), 13.

19   Ibid., 12.

20   Marian Christy, "Winning According to Schwarzenegger," *Boston Globe,* May 9, 1982.

21   Schwarzenegger, "The Education of an American" (speech, Perspectives 2001 Conference, Sacramento, September 21, 2001).

21   Todd Klein, "Arnold Schwarzenegger: More than Muscles," *Saturday Evening Post,* March 1988.

23   Schwarzenegger and Hall, *Arnold: The Education of a Bodybuilder,* 14.

24   Ibid., 17.

25   Schwarzenegger, "The Education of an American."

27–28   Schwarzenegger and Hall, *Arnold: The Education of a Bodybuilder,* 16.

29   Andy Eckardt, "Austrian Town Watches California Vote," *NBC Nightly News,* October 7, 2003.

30   Schwarzenegger and Hall, *Arnold: The Education of a Bodybuilder,* 27.

33   Ibid., 35.

33   Ibid., 34.

34   Ibid., 43.

37   Ibid., 47.

38   Ibid., 49.

39   Ibid., 58.

41–42   Ibid., 74.

42   Ibid., 77.

46   Ibid., 93.

49   Ibid., 104.

58   Schwarzenegger, "The Education of an American."

59   Schwarzenegger, "The Education of an American."

63   John L. Flynn, *The Films of Arnold Schwarzenegger* (New York: Citadel Press, 1993), 74.

65   Deirdre Donahue and Susan Reed, "A Hyannis Hitching," *People,* May 12, 1986.

68   Gerald Clarke, "New Muscle at the Box Office." *Time,* October 28, 1985.

68   Klein, "Arnold Schwarzenegger: More than Muscles."

70   Richard Corliss, "Box-Office Brawn," *Time,* December 24, 1990.

77   Marcus Errico, "Arnold Recovers from Heart Surgery," *E!Online,* April 16, 1997, <http://www.eonline.com/News /Items/0,1,974,00.html> (February 2004).

79 Karen Kornbluh, "The Parent Gap: What Arnold Schwarzenegger Can Teach Politicians about Winning Swing Voters," *Washington Monthly,* October 22, 2002.

79 Robert Kurson, "The Amazing Arnold! Part Two," *Esquire,* July 2003.

82 Schwarzenegger, interview by Jay Leno, *The Tonight Show,* NBC, August 6, 2003.

86 Judy Woodruff, Candy Crowley, and John Mercurio, "California Governor to Face Recall Vote," *CNN.com,* July 25, 2003, <http://www.cnn.com/2003/ALLPOLITICS /07/24/davis.recall/index.html> (March 2004).

86 John Mercurio, "California Recall Bid Succeeds," *CNN.com,* July 29, 2003, <http://www.cnn.com/2003/ALLPOLITICS /07/23/davis.recall/index.html> (March 2004).

87 "Schwarzenegger Follows Reagan's Path, Though Differences Abound," *abc7.com/KABC-TV,* Los Angeles, August 31, 2003, <http://abclocal.go.com/kabc/news /083103_nw_arnold_regan.html> (March 2004).

90 Ann Gerhart, "Can the Kennedys Embrace a Republican?" *Washington Post,* August 17, 2003.

90–91 William Booth and Dan Balz, "Schwarzenegger Goes for Outsider Role, Insider Help," *Washington Post,* September 4, 2003.

92 "62 Days that Reshaped a State: Schwarzenegger's Campaign," *abc7.com/KABC-TV,* Los Angeles, October 11, 2003, http://abclocal.go.com/kabc/news/101103_nw_recall _campaign.html> (March 2004).

96 Jim Wasserman, "Buoyed by Poll, Schwarzenegger Details Plan for First 100 Days in Office," *SFGate.com,* October 3, 2003, <http://www.sfgate.com/cgi-bin/article.cgi?file=/news/archive /2003/10/01/national1510EDT0679.DTL> (March 2004).

96 Gary Delsohn and Sam Stanton, "Day of Surprises: Schwarzenegger Says He's In," *Sacramento Bee,* August 7, 2003.

97 Charlie LeDuff and Adam Nagourney, "Schwarzenegger Goes into Defensive Mode," *New York Times,* October 3, 2003.

98 Candy Crowley, Frank Buckley, and Kelly Wallace, "Schwarzenegger Apologizes over Misconduct Allegations," *CNN.com,* October 3, 2003, <http://www.CNN.com> (October 2003).

99   LeDuff and Nagourney, "Schwarzenegger Goes into
     Defensive Mode."

99   Ibid.

99   Phil Hirschkorn, "Schwarzenegger Disputes Alleged Pro-
     Hitler Quote," *CNN.com*, October 3, 2003, <http://www
     .cnn.com/2003/ALLPOLITICS/10/03/schwarzenegger
     .hitler/index.html> (February 2004).

102 "Davis Concedes, Schwarzenegger Wins," *CNN.com*,
     October 8, 2003, <http://www.cnn.com/2003
     /ALLPOLITICS/10/07/recall.main/> (February 2004).

102 "Schwarzenegger: I Will Not Fail You."

103 Ibid.

103 Ibid.

SELECTED BIBLIOGRAPHY

Alter, Jonathan, and Karen Breslau. "Only in California."
     Newsweek, August 18, 2003.

Andrews, Nigel. *True Myths: The Life and Times of Arnold
     Schwarzenegger*, Secaucus, NJ: Birch Lane Press, 1977.

Arnold Schwarzenegger: The Official Web Site
     <http://www.schwarzenegger.com>

Booth, William, and Dan Balz. "Schwarzenegger Goes for Out-
     sider Role, Insider Help." *The Washington Post*, September 4,
     2003.

Christy, Marian. "Winning According to Schwarzenegger." *Boston
     Globe*, May 9, 1982.

Doherty, Craig A., and Katherine M. Doherty. *Arnold Schwarzenegger:
     Larger than Life*. New York: Walker and Company, 1993.

Donahue, Deirdre, and Susan Reed. "A Hyannis Hitching,"
     People, May 12, 1986.

Flynn, John L. *The Films of Arnold Schwarzenegger*. New York:
     Citadel Press, 1993.

Internet Movie Database: Arnold Schwarzenegger
     <http://www.imdb.com/name/nm0000216/>

Klein, Todd. "Arnold Schwarzenegger: More than Muscles."
  Saturday Evening Post, March 1988.
Schwarzeneger, Arnold. "The Education of an American." Speech,
  Perspectives 2001 Conference, Sacramento, September 21, 2001.
———. Interview by Jay Leno. *The Tonight Show,* NBC, August 6,
  2003.
Schwarzenegger, Arnold. *The New Encyclopedia of Modern
  Bodybuilding: The Bible of Bodybuilding.* New York: Simon
  and Schuster, 1999.
Schwarzenegger, Arnold, and Douglas Kent Hall. *Arnold: The
  Education of a Bodybuilder.* New York: Fireside, 1977.
"Schwarzenegger: I Will Not Fail You." *CNN.com,* October 8,
  2003.
Von Sternberg, Bob. "A Page from Ventura Script?" *Minneapolis
  Star Tribune,* October 9, 2003.

FOR FURTHER READING

Benson, Michael. *Ronald Reagan.* Minneapolis: Lerner
  Publications Company, 2004.
Donovan, Sandy. *Running for Office: A Look at Political
  Campaigns.* Minneapolis: Lerner Publications Company, 2004.
Hughes, Helga. *Cooking the Austrian Way.* Minneapolis: Lerner
  Publications Company, 2004.
Kennedy, Mike. *Special Olympics.* Danbury, CT: Children's Press, 2003.
Kowalski, Kathiann M. *Campaign Politics: What's Fair, What's
  Foul?* Minneapolis: Lerner Publications Company, 2000.
President's Council on Physical Fitness. <http://www.fitness.gov>.
  This website provides fitness, exercise, and nutrition
  information.
Schwarzenegger, Arnold, and Douglas Kent Hall. *Arnold: The
  Education of a Bodybuilder.* New York: Fireside, 1977.
Ventura, Jesse, and Herón Márquez. *Jesse Ventura Tells It Like It
  Is.* Minneapolis: Lerner Publications Company, 2002.

INDEX

OTHER TITLES FROM LERNER AND A&E®:

Arthur Ashe

The Beatles

Benjamin Franklin

Bill Gates

Bruce Lee

Carl Sagan

Chief Crazy Horse

Christopher Reeve

Colin Powell

Daring Pirate Women

Edgar Allan Poe

Eleanor Roosevelt

George W. Bush

George Lucas

Gloria Estefan

Jack London

Jacques Cousteau

Jane Austen

Jesse Owens

Jesse Ventura

Jimi Hendrix

John Glenn

Latin Sensations

Legends of Dracula

Legends of Santa Claus

Louisa May Alcott

Madeleine Albright

Malcolm X

Mark Twain

Maya Angelou

Mohandas Gandhi

Mother Teresa

Nelson Mandela

Oprah Winfrey

Osama bin Laden

Princess Diana

Queen Cleopatra

Queen Elizabeth I

Queen Latifah

Rosie O'Donnell

Saddam Hussein

Saint Joan of Arc

Thurgood Marshall

Tiger Woods

William Shakespeare

Wilma Rudolph

Women in Space

Women of the Wild West

Yasser Arafat

ABOUT THE AUTHOR

Colleen A. Sexton lives in Minnesota, where she has worked as an editor and writer for nearly fifteen years. A graduate of the College of St. Benedict in St. Joseph, Minnesota, she specializes in nonfiction books for children.

PHOTO ACKNOWLEDGMENTS

The images in this book are used with the permission of: © AFP/Getty Images, p. 2; © Kenneth James/CORBIS, p. 6; © Robert Galbraith/Reuters NewMedia Inc/CORBIS, p. 8; © Mark Richards/CORBIS, p. 9; © Getty Images, pp. 10, 14, 17, 22, 28, 43, 53, 72, 78, 89; © Michael Maloney/San Francisco Chronicle/CORBIS, pp. 11, 98; © Bruce Chambers/Orange County Register/CORBIS, p. 13; © Hollywood Book and Poster, pp. 20, 54, 62; © Hulton| Archive by Getty Images, pp. 24, 44; © Viennareport Agency/CORBIS SYGMA, p. 31; © CORBIS, p. 36; © Photofest, pp. 48, 61, 66, 69; © Time Life Pictures/Getty Images, pp. 57, 73; © Bettmann/CORBIS, p. 65; © Henry Diltz/CORBIS, p. 70; © Noecker Marcel/CORBIS SYGMA, p. 71; © Rufus F. Folkks/CORBIS, p. 76; © Reuters NewMedia Inc/CORBIS, pp. 80, 83; © Fred Prouser/Reuters NewMedia Inc/CORBIS, p. 86; © Michael Macor/San Francisco Chronicle/CORBIS, p. 91; © Frederic Larson/San Francisco Chronicle/CORBIS, p. 93; © Pool/Stephan Savoia/Reuters NewMedia Inc/CORBIS, p. 101; © Kenneth James/CORBIS, p. 102. Cover photos by Getty Images (both).

WEBSITES

Website addresses in this book were valid at the time of printing. However, because of the nature of the Internet, some addresses may have changed or sites may have closed since publication. While the author and Publisher regret any inconvenience this may cause readers, no responsibility for any such changes can be accepted by the author or Publisher.